INDIANA

ILLINOIS

Missouri River

Fort Leavenworth

Kansas River

Independence

Fort Osage

Arrow Rock

Franklin

Boon's Lick

St. Louis

Oregon Trail Junction

Council Grove

Osage River

MISSOURI

River

Osage River

Mississippi River

TENNESSEE

ARKANSAS

Arkansas River

OKLAHOMA

A Right Fine Life

KIT CARSON ON THE SANTA FE TRAIL

Andrew Glass

Holiday House/New York

My pappy followed Daniel Boone down the Wilderness Trail to Kentucky. Tweren't but two years before we moved on to Boon's Lick, Missouri. Pappy built a cabin and cleared some land. My big brothers, Andrew and Robert, came back from the West to help out. They told me stories of sights no greenhorn had yet laid eyes on. But as I wasn't sproutin' up tall and scrappy like them, Pappy set his hopes for me on book learning and sent me off to school.

"Maybe we can make a lawyer of ya, little man," he laughed. "Could be a proper refined life, lawyering."

When a tree fell on Pappy and kilt him, I set to working the farm like a grown man. Mama suggested I might best be a farmer like Pappy.

"Ya might yet make a decent enough life," she said, "right here in Boon's Lick." But when Mama got herself married again, I didn't take kindly to being treated like a hired hand by my new pa. That's how I come to be apprenticed to Mr. Workman in his saddler's shop, right smack on the edge of the western frontier in Franklin, Missouri.

From the shop window I watched folks with passels of younguns packing up prairie schooners for the hard trail northwest up to Oregon country. Traders were rigging their freight wagons, too, for the long dangerous trail to Santa Fe.

Mr. Workman was right fond of saying, "Franklin's gonna be a boomtown. Outfitting wagon trains could soon be a right prosperous enterprise." But rigging out other folks for adventures sure weren't my idea of living.

The first real mountain men I laid eyes on worked on the wagon trains as guides and buffalo hunters. Some were tough old buzzards with long, tangled beards. Others weren't much older than me.

I repaired their gear while they spun their far-fetched yarns. They showed me how to make a sheath for a skinning knife and a possibles bag for squirreling away any such thing as might come in handy. I made myself a fancy one from scraps, with my name tooled on the flap. I put a flint and a bit of iron, a button, an old needle, a length of string, and a sliver of soap inside.

"I'm ready to be a mountain man," I announced.

"That's a hoot, little Kit," they laughed. "Ha! Youngun," said Gabe. "Ya have pluck! But I don't reckon you'd last a day in the wild without a prodigious amount of luck."

They whacked each other on the back, laughing fit to be tied.

"If it's luck that's needed, I reckon I can make me some danged luck," I mumbled.

Just shy of my seventeenth birthday, I crossed the Missouri River by moonlight. With Pappy's old gun, Deadeye, over my shoulder, my possibles bag, and just the clothes on my back, I started out cross-country, eighty miles to Fort Osage.

I hired on with Captain Marshall's wagon train headed for Santa Fe.

"Your job's tending cavvy," the captain said. "Extra mounts, mares with skittish foals, half-broke horses, a few oxen, and some donkeys. Can ya handle that, boy?"

"Yes sir!" I answered.

That night I ate salt sowbelly and drank bitter coffee around a mess fire with traders, smugglers, mountain men, Delaware hunters, teamsters, and greenhorn sportsmen. There weren't any womenfolk along, nor littleuns, 'cause this was no settler's trail. The talk was about Comanches and prairie fires and a new fort along the Arkansas River. Traders, afeared for their wagons, spoke favorably of the new outpost.

But the mountain men grumbled. "Afore long the whole blamed country'll be lassoed with trails and brought to ruination."

I watched the mountain men turn in for the night and wrapped myself in a Mackinaw blanket and lay down on the hard ground with my rifle cradled in my arms, just like they did.

"Turn out!" the wagon master shouted.

In the shivery cold before dawn, I shook myself awake and rolled up my blanket.

"Catch up!" came the call to harness the wagons.

"All set!" was the final check.

"All set!" we called back.

"Then stre-e-e-e-etch out!" and the forty-two-odd wagons stretched out to the west. I kept cavvy together best I could through the choking, thick dust. I was half-starved by the time we stopped for breakfast at lunchtime. I figure we made maybe ten miles in a long, saddle-sore day. I felt grateful just to rest my bones on a rocky piece of ground.

Next day, I chose me a pony from the cavvy.

"He's a might puny, ain't he, Kit?" teamsters called out.

But he could turn pretty quick and steady, and he didn't spook easy. I named him Apache for his courage.

After Council Grove, the wild prairie commenced, and the wagons spread out, four across. Some days the wind blew so hard it near ripped the canvas off the wagons. Other days sudden rain fell in buckets. I learnt to push on, like a mule.

Bored mule skinners took to taking potshots at prairie wolves that skulked through high grass around the caravan. But I couldn't see the sport in it.

Mr. Broadus shot himself bad in the arm by accident, near shattered it. He bandaged it up and claimed he'd be all right. Said no one better touch him.

Soon thereafter, while chasin' down a particular lamebrained donkey and her wobbly foal, I noticed the pots and pans tinkling in the mess wagon. It weren't the usual clanking and banging neither. I felt a trembling rise right through my pony's hooves. Twisting round in the saddle, I saw a fearsome mountain of yellow dust and whirlwinds.

"Buffalo! Buffalo!" shouted the men, "headed this way!"

Greenhorn sportsmen grabbed their fancy guns and rode off shoutin' and shootin'. Even teamsters lost their heads and rode off, leavin' their mules buckin' and strainin' to break free. "Circle 'em!" barked Captain Marshall. "Drive 'em in hard! We won't never see 'em no more if they run off with the herd."

Axles squealed and terrified mules brayed. Men hollered and cursed. Huge, shaggy, horned buffalo broke wild-eyed through the thick dust cloud. Their hooves' poundin' made an awful roar. Spooked horses fell and riders jumped to save themselves. Dodging sharp horns, Apache lurched and stumbled and struggled to stay up.

"Stampede! Stampede! It's a prairie fire driving 'em," yelled teamsters.

Buffalo blundered past, pulling me farther from the wagons. I near took leave of my senses. Captain Marshall called out, "Kit!" but I was lost in the stampede.

I spotted the little donkey foal. Buffalo bulls, cows, and calves crashed past, near to trampling him under. I hoisted the donkey over my saddle. Bellowing beasts, scared crazy, fled from the leaping flames.

I broke from the herd and rode hard for the river, the fire near singeing my backside. Thunder crashed again. But it weren't buffalo this time. Thunderheads darkened the sky over the prairie fire. A blinding streak of lightning flashed and an earsplitting crash shook Heaven and Earth. Heavy drops fell in splats and hissed, dousing the flames.

With the next flash, I saw a ramshackle lean-to oft yonder in the smoldering prairie grass. As I spurred Apache through the storm, the hard rain turned to hail.

Just as I flung the shivering foal around my shoulders, I saw an Indian girl huddled behind a little grassy rise. She was holding tight to her spotted pony.

When she saw me fixin' to seek shelter in the shed, she shook her head and made signs.

I thought, *This crazy girl ain't got sense enough to come in outa the frozen rain.* So I stepped right around her.

"It's a lot drier in here," I called.

By the time I woke up, the storm had passed over. The ground smelled of wet burnt grass. Last thing I expected was to find the girl waiting for me, but there she was, soaked through and shivering a little. She looked up at me from under her eyebrows. The sun came out just as strong as before. I could feel steam rising from my soggy clothes, and I commenced to feeling a might itchy. Soon, I was scratching like a hound dog.

By the time my clothes dried, I knew I was covered with fleas—like tiny devils digging their pitchforks into me. Grinning wide, the girl watched me scratch and slap and hop and rub, just like I was part of some sorta travelin' show.

Finally, pity got the best of her, I guess, and she led me over to a bare anthill near the river. She signaled pretty clear for me to separate my clothes from my skin, toss the clothes onto the red-ant hill and myself into the river. I soaked and scrubbed with the sliver of soap from my possibles bag, while the fire ants made war on the fleas.

I was near scrubbed raw by the time she picked up my drawers, shook them free of all the ferocious red critters, and tossed them over to me. I pulled on the rest of my duds in a hurry.

I couldn't thank her proper, not speaking her language. Tweren't hardly just for showin' me a trick to relieve myself of a few fleas, neither. But for learning me that I'd best heed the wisdom of Indians if I hoped to live long in the wilderness. It was pure dumb luck that I hadn't busted in on a passel of rattlers.

I untied my possibles bag and presented it as I imagined a body would present a precious tribute to a princess. She accepted it just like a princess, too, serious and solemn.

"*Vih'hiu-nis,*" she said, touching my shoulder, like she was bestowing a grand title.

When she rode off, I considered what course I might best follow. I had no notion of where I might have got to. I'd heard tales of folks caught in the open, who wandered till they collapsed or got kilt. Even though I feared I might be trailing a fork in the river right into Apache country, my best hope was still to follow the treeless bank of the winding Arkansas. For just a moment, I had a notion that eternity might be like the wide prairie, stretching on forever and ever.

Countless buffalo trooped in columns along the horizon. Wolves watched me pass from the bottoms of ravines, and antelope leapt off as I came near. Snakes and lizards slithered away lazy-like. Whole villages of prairie dogs popped from their burrows to yelp at me. I felt just like old Adam himself, the first greenhorn at the beginning of the world, and I knew for certain I wanted to live in this world just the way the Good Lord made it: far from what folks call 'civilization,' and to have an adventure every day of my life.

"If I get out of this one," I promised out loud, "I'll learn the trail so well that folks will look to me to show them the way."

But for the ache in my stomach, I was near asleep in the saddle before I spotted the wagons stretched out to the southwest. Poor Apache was wore out, too. By the time we caught up, the wagon train was camped near a juttin' column of sandstone called Pawnee Rock.

Captain Marshall spotted me riding slow through the dry prairie grass. "I'm right glad to see ya back in one piece. You're a lucky feller, Kit Carson."

The moon hung over Pawnee Rock, while I feasted on red buffalo meat for the first time. Truth to tell, I couldn't recollect ever tasting anything quite so fine.

Mr. Broadus was doing right poorly, shivering in the firelight, his arm swole up something awful.

"Someone's gotta help him!" I said. "He's a sorry sight."

"That arm'll be the death of him, sure enough," replied a teamster.

I was sure hoping Captain Marshall would order someone to do something. But as he didn't seem inclined to, I felt a powerful itch to speak up.

"If someone who knows how won't do what has to be done," I said, "then I expect them that doesn't know will have to try."

"Meaning you, boy?" demanded Captain Marshall.

"Meaning me, sir," I answered.

"You're right, son," he said, "it's time we set to work." A grisly business it was, too. But Mr. Broadus woke up right pleased to be alive.

Some days later, Mr. Broadus leaned on me for support. "Captain Marshall told me how ya saw a vision, Kit, just like a young brave. That so?"

"Tweren't a vision, sir, just a girl," I said.

"Well, son, did your girl spirit give you a name?" he asked.

"Yes sir. She called me *Vih'hiu-nis*. Captain Marshall says it means 'Little Chief' in Cheyenne."

"I reckon that's the name for ya, too," he said. "You ain't sizable, but ya got the heart of a chief."

We were still a good ways from the end of the trail. I set to learnin' all I could as the wagons plodded west along the Arkansas River. We turned south at a place called Big Timbers, and rolled single file past abandoned Indian pueblos in the Sangre de Cristo Mountains. By the time the creaky wagons rolled down into Santa Fe, I was a pretty fair teamster.

Looking into the valley scattered with low adobe houses, I knew the end of the trail at Santa Fe was just the beginnin' for me. First chance I got, I'd head into the mountains. I was determined to have adventures before folks came to settle the wilderness and change it forever.

Writers of books wrote many a fanciful tale of my life as a mountain man. I believe some of the stories they told might even be true. I'm here to tell ya, it's been a right fine life.

ABOUT THE SANTA FE TRAIL

By the time Kit Carson ran away from Mr. Workman's saddler's shop in the fall of 1826, the wheel ruts in the prairie were already known as the Santa Fe Trail. Santa Fe was a commercial center for ranchers in New Mexico, which was then a colony of Spain. New Mexicans were anxious to buy Americans goods. Afraid of American influence over New Mexico, Spain made trade with any foreign country illegal. The only official trade route to Santa Fe was north from Chihuahua, Mexico. Mostly desert and mountains, it had to be traveled by pack train. By the time Spanish goods arrived, they were very expensive. Until 1821, any American caught on the Santa Fe Trail in Spanish territory was tossed into jail as a spy.

William Becknell, called the father of the Santa Fe Trail, set out on September 1, 1821, from Franklin, Missouri, with five frontiersmen he'd talked into risking their necks with him in the hope of big profits. They may have planned to trade knives and cotton cloth with the Osage Indians for buffalo robes and horses or mules stolen from the Spanish, just as other smugglers had done before. Or they may have planned to make the 870 mile trek to Santa Fe, figuring that if they got caught by the Spanish soldiers, they could claim to be trading with the Indians.

The group left the well-trodden trail along the Arkansas River at a little stream named Purgatoire, and followed the old trapper's trail to Santa Fe through the eastern foothills of the Sangre de Cristo Mountains. In the Raton Pass, they were surrounded by Mexican troops. The trading party spoke no Spanish and the soldiers spoke no English. Becknell expected to be put in irons. Instead, the soldiers communicated in signs that Mexico was finally free from Spain and that the traders were welcome to continue on to Santa Fe.

On November 16, Becknell and his men arrived in Santa Fe where they sold their goods at what seemed a huge profit to them but seemed cheap to the locals used to high prices. So everyone was happy.

Becknell, in a hurry to cash in on the new trade before others caught on, filled his saddle bags with silver and hurried back to Franklin. He cut the trip from seventy-seven days to forty-eight by taking the dry Cimarron River. Though he tried to keep his good fortune under his hat, the story goes that he was so loaded down with Spanish silver coins that they literally spilled onto the streets of Franklin.

Several other traders loaded up pack mules and headed for the mountain pass, hoping to make their fortunes, but Becknell had a better idea. He loaded three wagons, the first wagons ever used on the plains, and headed back. With only a hand compass to guide them, the party started across the Cimarron Desert. With their water gone after one day, animals died and men were collapsing, too. If the party hadn't come upon a buffalo, shot it, and drank the water in its stomach, the men never would have survived. Indians harassed them, and stampeding buffalo scattered the mules and horses; but when the party finally arrived in Santa Fe, they sold everything, including the wagons. The Santa Fe Trail was officially a road.

Becknell and his party opened up the trail to Conestoga wagons built by Dutch settlers in the Conestoga Valley of Pennsylvania. Nicknamed prairie schooners, they were the most commonly used wagon on the trail between 1820 and 1840. The boat-shaped body carried a load of glassware, shoes, cloth, clothing, buttons, buckles, shovels, axes, coffee, gunpowder, soap, scissors, nails, knives, and other hardware toward its center, making it more stable on rough roads or sloping mountain passes. Heavily loaded prairie schooners traveling in large caravans were easier to defend against Indians or outlaws. But rockslides, heat, dust clouds, lightning storms, prairie fires, stampedes, and even mirages posed threats. Accidents, too, took many lives.

Eight mules, driven by a mule skinner, were needed to pull a prairie schooner. Mules were much tougher than horses but unpredictable and difficult to manage. Mule skinners became legendary for brutality, foul language, and long mustaches. Oxen were introduced in 1829 because they were cheaper than mules. These Missouri steers, with their large hooves, pulled better and could graze along the trail. American Indians weren't interested in stealing oxen, and if an unlucky wagon train encountered no buffalo, the men could eat them. Oxen were driven by well-paid bullwhackers, who didn't whip the beasts but popped the whips over the oxen's heads. Buffalo hunters came along to supply meat and drive off the large, shaggy herds.

The wagons plodded along in four parallel columns after reaching Council Grove, Kansas, 150 miles west of Independence, Missouri. This formation discouraged attacks and made it easier to form a circle for protection. Wagon trains made their best time in the cool of the morning, stopping for breakfast after four hours on the trail, cooking on fires of buffalo chips when no wood could be found. At night they took turns standing guard outside the corral of wagons.

Once the Bent brothers built a fort on the Arkansas River and widened the Raton Pass in 1834, the Cimarron Pass was seldom used. New Mexico was proclaimed a territory of the United States in 1846, and trade increased to supply the new Americans. By 1880 the first train chugged through the Raton Pass and south into Santa Fe, forever replacing covered wagons.

ABOUT KIT CARSON

Kit Carson's father, Lindsey Carson, was born in 1754, fought in the American Revolution, and followed Daniel Boone down the Wilderness Trail to Kentucky. Christopher Houston Carson, called "Kit," was born December 24, 1809, in Madison County, Kentucky. Before Kit was two years old, the family moved on to Boon's Lick, Missouri. Kit had four half brothers and two half sisters, five full brothers and four full sisters. There were more to come when his mother remarried after his father died.

Since Kit was small and showed some intellectual promise, his father sent him off to school. But the story goes that one day American Indians attacked the settlement, and Kit dropped his spelling book on the dirt floor of the schoolhouse, grabbed up his pappy's old flintlock, Deadeye, ran to help defend the farm, and never set foot in school again. Kit never learned to read or write, though he later worked as a translator, having learned to speak Spanish, French, and many languages of the American Indians, including the sign language of the Plains tribes.

His father was crushed by a falling tree in 1818. After that, Kit shouldered the work on the farm. Robert and Andrew returned from the West to help. Another brother, Moses Carson, had worked as a trapper on the Missouri River.

When Kit's mother remarried in 1821, Kit was apprenticed to Mr. Workman's saddler's shop on the edge of the western frontier in Franklin, Missouri. That's where he first saw real mountain men who worked as guides and buffalo hunters. They dressed in fringed buckskin and beaded moccasins, nearly passing for the American Indians they so admired. Mountain men depended on the generosity and knowledge of the American Indians for their survival.

From the shop window, Kit saw traders forming the first large caravan to Santa Fe. They packed goods in layers with blankets to cushion them in the huge wagons. Some hollowed out axles where they hoped to hide Mexican silver.

In 1826 Kit joined up with the second big wagon train. When Kit ran away, Mr. Workman placed a notice in the local paper, as he was required to do by law if an apprentice broke his contract. So Kit had a price on his head, but the reward was only one penny. His understanding boss even printed misleading information, indicating that the runaway had gone north.

In recounting his first trip to Santa Fe, Kit particularly recalled the shooting accident and primitive operation that saved Andrew Broadus's life.

From Santa Fe, Kit went on to Taos to be near the mountains and beaver country. Kit roamed throughout the West as a fur trapper. He gained an unparalleled knowledge of the geography and wildlife of the West that enabled him to survive in the wilderness where many others failed. He respected the cultures and learned the languages of many of the Western tribes. Kit remembered his days as a free trapper as the best years of his life, full of dangers but without the responsibilities of leadership. He doesn't seem to have sought out leadership, though it later fell upon him.

Fur hats went out of fashion and the beaver were depleted by overtrapping. After years in the mountains, it became impossible for Kit to make a living as a free trapper. His exceptional skill and extensive knowledge of the West and its people made Kit a legendary guide, scout, and hunter.

Kit had three wives. The first was an Arapaho woman named Waa-nibe, with whom he had two daughters. One daughter died very young. After Waa-nibe died, Kit was briefly married to a Cheyenne woman named Making-out-road. He took his first wife's daughter, Adaline, and returned to Missouri, leaving her with his sister Mary Ann. Later Kit married Senorita Josefa Jaramillo and settled in Taos.

In 1842 John C. Frémont, nicknamed the Pathfinder, hired Kit as a guide on an official trip to map the Rocky Mountains. For the next four years, Kit guided Frémont on three expeditions through the Western wilderness.

The reports of Frémont's expeditions inspired people to go west and depicted Kit as the guide to the Pathfinder. Stories told around campfires made Kit famous. Ten-cent novels made him a hero among boys, while growing numbers of believers in Manifest Destiny, the divine right of America to expand, credited frontiersmen such as Kit with being leaders of the movement.

In 1846, during Kit's third expedition with Frémont to the Great Salt Lake, he was caught up in the war with Mexico. He was promoted to brigadier general during the Indian Wars in the Southwest. In the early days, the tribes traded with mountain men; they trapped together, and trappers married American Indian women. But as the traders and settlers began to kill or scare off the buffalo, cut down trees, and bring terrible diseases like smallpox, the tribes began attacking the wagon trains and forts. In 1856 Kit became an Indian agent, attempting to keep peace between the tribes and protect them from corrupt politicians. In 1863 he led 700 men in what was known to settlers as the "bloodless" campaigns against more than 8,000 Apaches, Comanches, and Navajos, forcing them to surrender and return to the reservations by destroying their crops and livestock. Many died on the long march to the reservations. The treatment of American Indians casts a shadow over the lives of all who were touched by it. Kit Carson, though he loved the Indian way of life, helped to destroy it. As a soldier, Kit was caught in the politics of claiming land for settlers and fortune hunters. However, as an Indian agent in northern New Mexico, the tribes considered Kit one of the few white men they could trust to look out for their interests. He was given his name, *Vih'hiu-nis,* by a Cheyenne chief. He died in the Colorado territory in 1868—the year the great slaughter of the once vast buffalo herds began—while serving as Superintendent of Indian Affairs. He is buried with his wife in Taos, New Mexico, the town he thought of as his home.

Author's Note

Like many heros and heroines, Kit Carson's real life was obscured by legend. Pulp-fiction writers fabricated tales of his adventures, and Kit Carson biographies were based more on legend than actual accounts. Books referring to those earlier books presented the legendary information as fact. It all makes for an interesting muddle.

My purpose in writing this story is to tell a tall tale like those the old mountain men typically told around the campfire, putting the teller of the tale right smack in the middle as the hero of his own story.

SELECTED BIBLIOGRAPHY

Carter, Harvey Lewis. *Dear Old Kit.* Norman, OK: University of Oklahoma Press, 1968.
Garst, Shannon. *Kit Carson: Trail Blazer and Scout.* New York: Julian Messner, Inc., 1942.
Hoffman, Wilber. *Sagas of Old Western Travel and Transport.* San Diego, CA: Howell North Publishers, 1968.
Lavender, David. *The Santa Fe Trail.* New York: Holiday House, 1995.
Moody, Ralph. *Kit Carson and the Wild Frontier: The Life and Adventures of Kit Carson.* New York: Random House, 1955.
Vestel, Stanley. *Kit Carson.* Boston: Houghton Mifflin, 1928.

For my mother.

Library of Congress Cataloging-in-Publication Data
Glass, Andrew, 1949–
A right fine life : Kit Carson on the Santa Fe Trail / Andrew
Glass. — 1st ed.
p.   cm.
Summary: Shortly before his sixteenth birthday, Kit Carson leaves
his home in Missouri, heads out for Santa Fe, and begins a series of
adventures as a legendary mountain man.
ISBN 0-8234-1326-8
1. Carson, Kit, 1809–1868—Juvenile fiction.   [1. Carson, Kit,
1809–1868—Fiction.   2. West (U.S.)—Fiction.]   I. Title.
PZ7.G481155Ri   1997   97-10949   CIP   AC
[Fic]—dc21

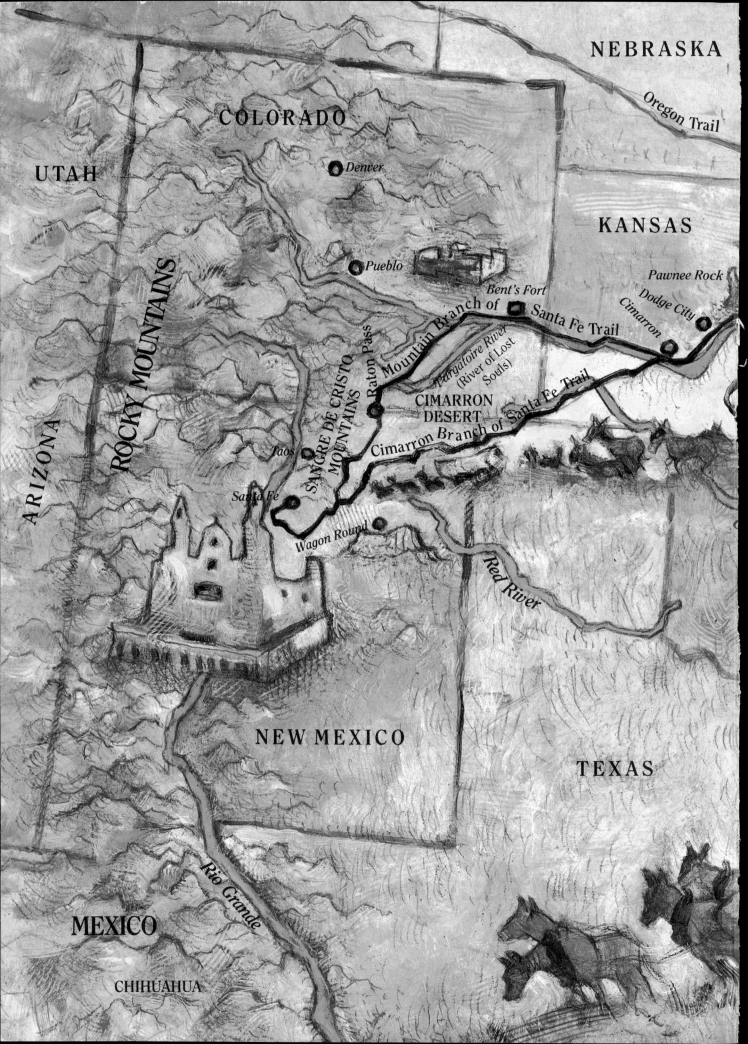